D0761139

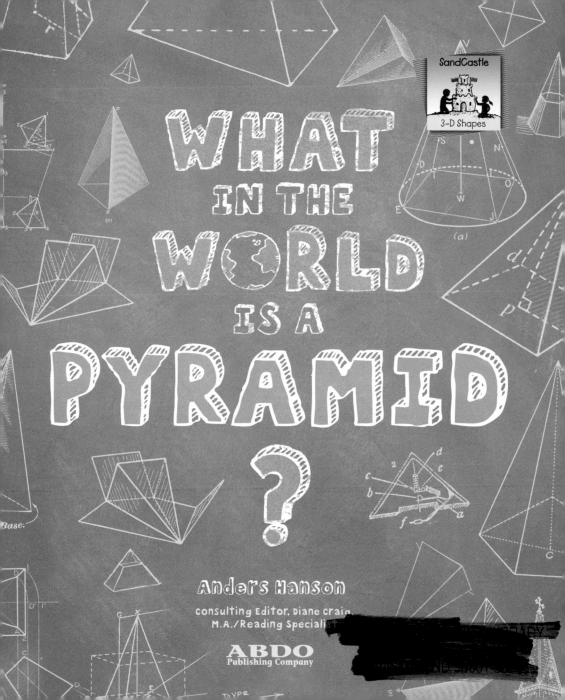

SandCastle

3-D Shapes

WHAT IN THE WORLD IS A PYRAMID?

Anders Hanson

Consulting Editor, Diane Craig,
M.A./Reading Specialist

ABDO
Publishing Company

Published by ABDO Publishing Company, 8000 West 78th Street, Edina, MN 55439.

Copyright © 2008 by Abdo Consulting Group, Inc. International copyrights reserved in all countries.

No part of this book may be reproduced in any form without written permission from the publisher.
SandCastle™ is a trademark and logo of ABDO Publishing Company.

Printed in the United States.
Editor: Pam Price
Curriculum Coordinator: Nancy Tuminelly
Cover and Interior Design and Production: Mighty Media
Photo Credits: JupiterImages Corporation, ShutterStock

Library of Congress Cataloging-in-Publication Data

Hanson, Anders, 1980-
  What in the world is a pyramid? / Anders Hanson.
    p. cm. -- (3-D shapes)
  ISBN-13: 978-1-59928-890-1
  1. Pyramid (Geometry)--Juvenile literature. 2. Shapes--Juvenile literature. 3. Geometry, Solid--
Juvenile literature. I. Title.
  QA491.H3665 2007
  516'.156--dc22
                          2007015624

SandCastle™ books are created by a team of professional educators, reading specialists, and content developers around five essential components—phonemic awareness, phonics, vocabulary, text comprehension, and fluency—to assist young readers as they develop reading skills and strategies and increase their general knowledge. All books are written, reviewed, and leveled for guided reading, early reading intervention, and Accelerated Reader® programs for use in shared, guided, and independent reading and writing activities to support a balanced approach to literacy instruction. The SandCastle™ series has four levels that correspond to early literacy development. The levels are provided to help teachers and parents select appropriate books for young readers.

SandCastle™ Level: Transitional

Emerging Readers
(no flags)

Beginning Readers
(1 flag)

Transitional Readers
(2 flags)

Fluent Readers
(3 flags)

SandCastle™ would like to hear from you. Please send us your comments or questions.

sandcastle@abdopublishing.com

3-D shapes are all around us.

3-D stands for 3-dimensional.

It means that an object is not flat.

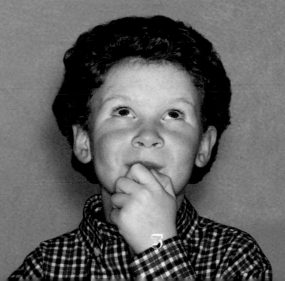

A pyramid is a 3-D shape.

APEX ←

BASE

A pyramid has an apex
and a polygonal base.

The base and the apex are joined by triangular faces.

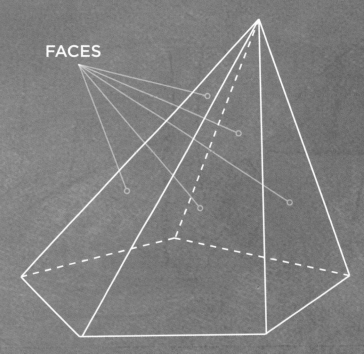

FACES

The number of faces equals the number of sides of the base.

Pyramids are everywhere!

The Great Pyramid of Giza is the only one of the seven wonders of the ancient world that still exists.

A glass pyramid serves as the main entrance to the famous Louvre Museum in Paris.

This three-sided
toy pyramid is
made up of many
smaller pyramids.

11

A pyramid has
a wide base. It
gets smaller
toward the apex.

It is easy to
stack objects in
a pyramid shape.

Some skyscrapers are shaped like pyramids.

The Transamerica Pyramid is the tallest building in San Francisco.

The back of
the U.S. dollar
bill shows a
pyramid broken
into two parts.

This pyramid is
made of sand
and seashells.

Have you ever
made a pyramid?

Find the pyramid!

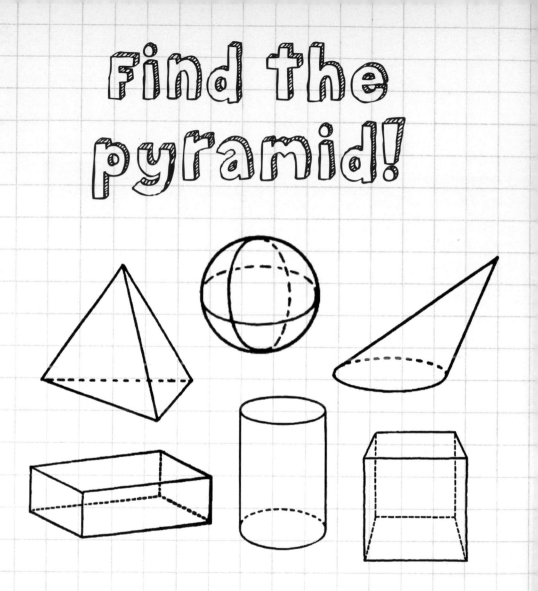

Which one of these 3-D shapes is a pyramid?

How many pyramids can you find in this photo?

Everyday pyramids

Take a look around you.

Do you see any pyramids?

How to draw a pyramid

1. Draw two lines that share an endpoint.

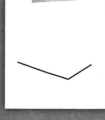

2. Draw a point above the lines.

3. Connect the endpoints of the lines to the point.

Glossary

ancient - very long ago or very old.

apex - the highest point.

base - the side or face on which a 2-D or 3-D figure can rest.

dimensional - having a measurement of length, width, or thickness.

endpoint - a point at the end of a line segment or a ray.

polygonal - having a two-dimensional shape with any number of sides and angles.

To see a complete list of SandCastle™ books and other nonfiction titles from ABDO Publishing Company, visit www.abdopublishing.com.

8000 West 78th Street, Edina, MN 55439 · 800-800-1312 · 952-831-1632 fax

HISTORICAL MUSEUM